AF505761

Fiction

The Reason for Crows, a novel of Kateri Tekakwitha
Pushing the Bear, After the Trail of Tears
Stone Heart, a novel of Sacajawea
Designs of the Night Sky
The Mask Maker
The Man Who Heard the Land
Fuller Man
Flutie
Pushing the Bear
The Only Piece of Furniture in the House
The Dance Partner, Stories of the Ghost Dance
The Voice That Was in Travel
Monkey Secret
Firesticks
Trigger Dance

Nonfiction

In-between Places
The Cold-and-Hunger Dance
The West Pole
Claiming Breath

Poetry

Asylum in the Grasslands
Rooms, New and Selected Poems
Primer of the Obsolete
The Shadow's Horse
The Stones for a Pillow
The Relief of America
Coyote's Quodlilbet
(Ado)ration
Boom Town
Lone Dog's Winter Count
Iron Woman
Offering
One Age in a Dream
Brown Wolf Leaves the Res

Drama

The Sum of Winter and other plays www.alexanderstreet.com
American Gypsy
War Cries

STORIES OF
THE DRIVEN WORLD

by

DIANE GLANCY

Mammoth Publications
Lawrence, Kansas 66044-4540

ISBN 978-0-9800102-9-9

Published by Mammoth Publications, Lawrence

Distributed by Mammoth Publications
1916 Stratford Rd., Lawrence, KS 66044
mammothpubs@hotmail.com
www.mammothpublications.com

Cover painting by Thomas Pecore Weso. Inquiries should be directed to Mammoth Publications.

Permission from Copper Canyon Press, www.coppercanyonpress.org, to
   reprint Eleanor Rand Wilner's excerpt from "Field of Vision," *The Girl
   with Bees in Her Hair*, © 2004 by Eleanor Rand Wilner
Permission to use the Peter Blue Cloud excerpts from *Elderberry Flute Song*,
   from Dennis Maloney, editor, White Pine Press, Lake View, New York
Permission to quote from *How Early America Sounded*, Richard Cullen Roth,
   Cornell University Press, Ithaca, New York
Acknowledgment to Sun and Moon Press, Los Angeles, for the excerpts
   from *The Confetti Trees*, 1999
Barbara Guest excerpts from "The Cough," The Vanished Library,"
   "Nostalgia," and "The Tear," from *The Collected Poems of Barbara Guest*, ©
   2008 by The Estate of Barbara Guest and reprinted by permission of
   Wesleyan University Press.

ACKNOWLEDGMENTS

Chaffin Journal for "By saying this I am saying"
Colere for "Waxed Cylinder"
Divide, Pax Americana for "I set forth my mission"
Ginko Tree Review for "The Dock"
In Posse Review for "Absalom, the Long Hair"
Iron Horse Literary Review for "Comet"
Isotope, a Journal of Literary Nature and Science Writing for "Vixen"
Kenyon Review for "He Lived in a Time of Weather"
Margie, the American Journal of Poetry for "The farther north I traveled the colder it got"
Pedestal Magazine for "Vision Quest at the Comet Motel"
Pilgrimage for "Wigwamming" and "Parking in the Village"
Poetry Daily, www.poems.com, 2/11/2010, for "He Lived in a Time of Weather"
Poetry NZ for "Wyandotte County Historical Society and Museum" and "I ask about seal hunting"
Red Dirt for "Afterburn"
Shenandoah for "Pictograph Caves Near Billings" and "The Legacy of Plains Indian Shirts"
Spare Mule for "Suite for Snowplow"
Steam Ticket for "The Capitalistic Notebooks"
The Christian Century for "Pumice"
The Traveling Elements, edited by Anita Endrezze and Lulu Kelly, a bookworks collage of painting and poetry, for "Iowa Migration Wetland, Late Winter"
Washington Square for "Voices from the driven world (1)," "Ethnology Drawer #2 File 145," "The Pillion" and "They wouldn't stay dead"
Water-Stone for "Donner and Blitzen"
Yellow Medicine River for "Paul Bunyan Series"
Native American Voices on Identity, Art and Culture, Objects of Everlasting Esteem: Masterpieces from the Collections of the University of Pennsylvania Museum, University of Pennsylvania Museum Press, 2005, for "Combs Cherokee"
Poetry Daily, www.poems.com, 2/25/05, for "Pictograph Caves Near Billings"
Ghost of a Chance, Gloria Vando and Philip Miller, editors, Helicon Nine Editions, for "Ethnology Drawer #2 File 145"
Unraveling the Spreading Cloth of Time: Indigenous Thoughts Concerning the Universe, edited by Marijo Moore, for "Birch bark biting"

Grateful acknowledgement also to the National Endowment for the Arts
Acknowledgment to Gove Hill Center, Vermont, and the Johnson County Library, Overland Park, Kansas, for first readings.

This book is for Ray

CONTENTS

CAPITALISTIC NOTEBOOKS

WIGWAM SERIES

FIELD REPORT

EPILOGUE

A frantic ethnographer out of his element.

The indigenous struggle to understand the new civilization

with its logging camps, eight reindeer and Christianity.

STORIES OF THE DRIVEN WORLD is an exploration of

the ethnographer's sometimes disjointed fieldnotes

and the questioning of those he came to document.

From pictograph to contemporary film-making

STORIES OF THE DRIVEN WORLD examines

a confrontation of cultures,

each one longing for answers to roll onto the horizon

like the morning sun.

Pictograph Caves Near Billings

Among the yellowed fields, the sumac thickets,
the hide of rolling hills, the cliffs,
and in them, caves where ancient ones
left drawings of animals, hunters, the usual ceremony for survival.
This graffiti, this old library. A story the grasses pick up,
and the leaf rattling across the ground like a snake repeats.

It is hard to imagine the firelight
that brought the animals and hunters to life, the hunger
that charged the brain with a vision
of the world in a different light.
Now interpretive markers under glass: What needs to be *explained?*
The spear into animal; the kill to feed.
The pictographs drew power from the rock walls of the caves.

Along the top of the cliffs, the rows of trees are hunters returning.

There are cottonwoods along the creek,
sparse clumps of trees on hills, black-veined coal in the cut-bank;
elsewhere, the clayed gray-green soil.

There's a low rumble of distance, of space,
while wind talks to the trees
long before my father worked in the stockyards
and my mother stood beside him in a slinky dress
the First Maker dug these caves to hide from the cries of hunger,
the stomp of drums, when the ancient ones came
to the cliffs for ceremony.
This was when the rock had voice, the birds and animals,
the wild rose, harebell, star flower, chokecherry,
the *grapey* current, the buffalo berry, all of them,
joined to tell stories for shelter, for company.

Later that day I fly in a small plane from Billings to Havre
over tanned fields, the dark slits of soil,
the gullies in the mounds of land
catching shadows in the low sun as the plane banks

for its stop in Lewiston on the way to Havre in the old peace
of evening before the night stalkers, the veins of hunger.

Then the plane lifts again, this time into dark, and I,
the only passenger now, have to sit alone, center, back,
as if in my room.
And, shortly, through the windshield, far ahead,
because the cock-pit door is open,
I see the runway lights in Havre.

It is written here, the old story, the first lesson: the darkness
needed to uncover those lights blue as rows of cornflowers
in my mother's yard
when turbulence rocks the small plane in a sudden crosswind
where ancient ones draw the last flight of the day
pulling out the Maker's power buried in the rock,
aligning weapon with animal on the cave wall, saying,
this is the way it has been when the spear was sent
into the animal in the hunt,
and the plane makes its way to the landing.

Birch bark biting

A metaphoric alignment is close to
what birch bark biting is because it
gets behind the edge of what can
be reached, which is where it
arrives and parts from as well.
Birch bark biting is an indention of
this. In birch bark biting, the teeth
indent a pattern of some sort on a
peeled strip of birch bark. The
birch bark is folded twice (the
same principle used in making
paper dolls). The bitten is usually a
floral pattern. Afterwards the bark
is unfolded from the biting. Often,
the teeth wear out from so much
biting. Eventually there are birch
bark bitings made by dentures.
Though birch bark biting is done
by a northern tribe, the Cherokee
could define it *a-wa-da-n'-toh'-ta-nv*
(my former tooth toothed by me)
and / or *u-da-n'-toh-ta-nv* (a tooth
separate from its body), which is
the etching or indention of tooth
marks on the bark. It's native
theory— there's a connection
between birch bark biting and the
mystery in the center of the
unification theory. Birch bark
biting is an active state, simple yet
quandrous, with the question of how
you get from tooth to pattern in
the time-space arena between the
cosmological constant and the
uncertainty principle.

Le ne'ha' na nesh   in che' on gee lang   ya'nee
All/   persons/   deer/   went after/ they say/

Sah doong ha' ts kaL   ya'nee
Alone/   [s]he walked/ they say./

Karl Kroeber, "The Man Eater," *An Introduction to the Art of Traditional American Indian Narration. Traditional Literature of the American Indian, Texts and Interpretations*

Absalom, the Long Hair[1]

A message came saying the last leaf had
fallen from the tree.
    Afterwards he slept disturbed by dreams.
    He stretches out the heavens as a tent.[2]
They stand up together clattering the
tent stakes.
    His wife, tired of hanging over a dark
space, slept in another room.
    He rode his mule under the blue leaves
suspended in trees. [Maybe Dakota ghost
shirts printed with blue hands—but no,
that was still ahead. The tribes (where did
they know trees on the open prairie?) wore
ghost-dance shirts Custer wouldn't live to
see.[3] Blue hands grew from their stems.
Osage Chief Bacon Rind. The Comanche.
Kiowa. Shoshoni. The Cheyenne camps.
They rode head-on into the oak (the ghost
of the 7th calvary, no he meant cavalry) (the
closeness of those 4-drive words!).]
    Nightmares running, shouting. Dreams
with thick boughs in them. A giant oak
caught Absalom's head in the fork of its
low branch. Suspended between the heaven
and earth, the mule under him went away.
    Before the massacre, his wife baked
five-pointed hands covered with blue icing.
    He cut the legs off his straight-back
chair. Cut the legs off one side of the table.
Painted the table blue. A ramp for skate
board or roller blade. Or make-shift stage.

---

[1] II Samuel 14:26 When Absalom, David's son, cut his hair, it weighted 200 shekels. Long Hair also was a name given by Indians to General George Custer
[2] Isaiah 40:22
[3] Custer died in the 1876 Battle of the Little Bighorn. The Ghost Dance would end at the Massacre at Wounded Knee, December 29, 1890

Not the way he would open the Indian wars
(no, they were still ahead) or even a road show,
the tent stakes clapping.

The frisbee of all those scalps, he said
in the crudest terms.

Isn't it in the hereafter they eat as many
cookies as they like?

The Iron Horse rumbled on the prairie
where Absalom danced from his tree, a
marionette with hands looping the air.

Absalom brained his rack. He ghost
danced his nightmares. He dreamed at the
mercy seat of rebellion.

[In 1942, prisoners of war built a
railroad from Burma to Thailand so Japan
could invade India. The prisoners suffered
cholera, dysentery, beriberi and ulcerated
sores deep as bone. Every night they
performed plays to keep themselves alive.
Every play had a train.]

The soldiers thrust three arrows into
the heart of A.

The chair seat flying like a saucer with
the runged back of an instrument panel, or
a much larger frisbee flying above the
compacted fragments of the stage [which a
train is.]

I set forth my mission (1)

It is not easy. It never was. To go
out among them with my pencil
and notebook, my straw hat in the
rain, and say, tell me your stories,
and I tell you they did. At first,
before they were suspicious, they
spoke. The translator said they did
anyway and I wrote with ease.[4]
Just because they live here a while
they think they own the land.
Where is their bill of sale? The
ownership papers? The abstract?
The title? It is here a salmon came
out of the water and stood on its
tail and spoke as if a chief reading a
speech he himself had written. His
scales were made of trade beads
and his eyes the sparks of rippling
water. He said the river was his to
give and he gave it to them, as if
the river could be given by a fish.
A fish I tell you, that's what they
think. A salmon with ownership.
Could it take notes with a pencil
behind its ear? Could he call the
salmon back? I ask to clarify the
issue (?), but the translator said the
salmon was from the spirit world
and could not be called, but
happened of its own will. How do
differences meet? How do we see
one another from the forest that is
ourselves we must see through?
How does anyone meet another
and converse and understand? If

---

[4] Speech patterns sounding like: __ |` |` __`| __ |` __`

anything, my fieldwork, my field
journeys, my field journals— I am
writing in sinkers and hipboots
from the rivulets wherein I stand
overwhich or whereover the birds
fly and squawk— the birch and
larch and trees in general because I
couldn't think of anymore names.

In which I continue to ponder (2)

One of them with a goiter said
[something large at his neck] he
was a part-ghost part-man who
walks two worlds not sure himself
which one he's in. I see him
checking his map, holding a wet
finger to the air, a windsock on his
arm for a sleeve. But these are the
stories I came to write, I remind
myself. Over and over, I wet my
pencil on my tongue and give them
another page pure and troubled as
the breath of a cloud and from as
far up. They act as if we sublet.
Their names Turtum and
Gwa'lafax [the goitered one] do
most of the speaking now *whox't* |
n'otb | *wto'ba* | *cax'two*. I don't
question but write who knows
what. The interpreter [I have
another one now] said they said,
you see there are few of us here in
Git'anmkes' but the Nibo'x'htas
spoke with their tongues and it was
hard to follow. They were what I
could call inhospitable spitting out
their words without giving me time
to write.[5] What were they angry
about? I am here to record. To
preserve. Do they want extinction?
Do they want to disappear without
a trace? *gax'lk* | *xigim'we* | *g'* is the
closest I can make of their
language [their fortified fort]
wherein they dwell

---

[5] | |_ | |`| | | | |`| | | |_ | | |`

into which I take my notebook and
walk their wet fields and rivulets.
They became more remote, less
open, wanted more for their stories
each time I went. Gwa'lafax and
Hala'max, whom he said now was
his brother, and Turtum, whom I
myself had grown to mistrust, gave
sounds as if wanting me to leave
before lifting their totem pole with
the help of something— the
salmon in galoshes I suppose.

I ask about seal hunting

I thought it would be simple but
they kept spilling out words like
stones marking nowhere. Dog
sleds, sledges, the drifting ice
packs. You don't know how
disconcerting. The fractions of
language. Epidemics killed most.
Alcohol renders the rest useless.
They count by means of fingers
and toes. A man when he gets to
twenty is *a man brought to the end of
himself.* Where am I now, oh yes, I
record:
bearded seal not a year old *qasEraq*
bearded seal one-year-old *am'iAq*
bearded seal more than one *ukjuk*
speckled seal of any age *qasigiAq*
fijord seal *nacEq*
old stinking ringed seal *tixak*
hunting seal on winter ice *siko*
hunting seal on thin ice *sa'l'raq*
hunting seal on year-old ice that has been blown *pEruliat*
hunting seal on ice without snow *uagsisaq*
hunting seal on pack ice *maneiAq*
catching seal *anuvcq*
catching seal at breathing hole *niqparpcq*
catching seal creeping on the ice *acrpcq*
catching seal from kayak *raqipcqppppppppppppppppp*
catching seal from chair for ice hunting *prrcprca*
catching seal when cold
catching seal with storm approaching
catching seal when family cries with hunger
I can write only so long I begin to
lose track could they slow down? I
copy repetitions til I flense.

The farther north I traveled the colder it got

The cold— I was afraid of it I tell
you— it was not a course I wanted
to stay on— just take my notes and
board the freighter back. There
was something— an unfriendly
edge in the air— it spooked the
moisture. You could see your
breath take the form of a ghost. It
was so cold these Eskimos could
find their way across the ice spread
everywhere. They knew where they
were going they could have left me
stranded and lost with my
companion the cold, the ice— I
talked to it on nights my teeth
chattered. These Eskimos take
stones or small rocks and make a
path across the ice— they could
find their way as I said across what
would lose anyone else. Sometimes
the Eskimos laid the stones in
circles and the caribou always
curious would enter and there be
killed or captured. BEWARE I
wrote the caribou of large circles of
stones— don't walk into the corral
of an Eskimo— BeWare you
caribou— you know who you
are— how could I make them
understand with this iceberg on my
arm— this icefield for a sleeve.

Disparities of the Driven World

I tried to preserve [them] for the
new world but they were reluctant
retreating to their villages their
blubber-oil lamps their smudge on
everything. I grew weary
depressed I could hardly lift my
head they lifted for me / poured
whatever it was they said into a cup
/ those who didn't want me here /
their heads appeared in the ice-
block igloo: they could see a *snout
animal* they said / a few short tusks
in its mouth / ears on its nose / an
animal covered with loops / its
head merely jaws / other restless
spirits Nalaqnaq and Kigutilik they
drew for me moving at a run /
large bumps at the joints / those
apprehensions / apparitions / and
seeings not there / I lost my verve
my snap my progress [get this
snow out of my face] this thought
grafted onto what? I grew
SPOOKED at the ice ridges
couldn't get my sled across abrupt
changes shifts in weather the cold
the cold the unrelenting handle on
the hard pump of darkness.

Waxed Cylinder

My father did his most excellent
work among the tribes. His second
wife [not my mother] turned them
over to us on his death [she felt
they weren't of use]. She gave us
what she didn't understand [didn't
want] his field work among the
natives recording not one tribe but
moved among many sometimes
before complete. Postcards from
places [we got out the map] my
mother with children could not
follow. Some of them were
undernotes *we* couldn't understand.
Among them letters written to him
we don't know from whom. The
fieldnotes were more about the
man than the work she said. We
continue to disseminate.

Prescription Sticks[6]

They look like a row of winter
trees scratched on wood that could
be a rung on the back of a straight-
back chair— *YYYY*— something
like that I'm trying to take these
notes— what do you expect when
I don't know what these things
mean / these markings / these
scratches made by a superstitious
people— I am left to the powers
of my own observations— they
made these primitive prayer sticks
/ prescription sticks— whatever
they called them— they thought
they formed the happenings in the
world by their scratchings / their
cross-files / their cross-fields /
their cross-fires / they maybe stole
/ they could not have thought
something like that up.[7]

---

[6] The Nelson-Atkins Museum of Art, Kansas City
[7] *Take a stick and write on it—* Ezekiel 37:16

A letter among his papers

This correspondence is to inform
that our people are hungry / we
were promised rations and rotten
by the time they arrive if they
arrive. Often there is nothing I say
/ I'm not sure what this will spur /
we are grateful for your visit / we
are glad you asked for our words
which we told. We could see you
took down what we said / we
could see you wrote. We have
nothing to give but hold out our
empty hands and say the loaves
and fishes you told us about don't
seem to pontiferate this far north.

STORIES OF THE DRIVEN WORLD:
(1) THE DEER RIDER

> Deer bore them on their backs.
>
> Montezuma

Donner and Blitzen

Beating the oxen never worked.
They traveled their same pace.
Other storms would concede but
this one took ox, horse, dog,
the boiled hides of animals,
shoe leather,
then some of their own
kind.
The argument with sky, tree, wind
over who subdues
decentered their world.
The wind brutal as the whip.
Birds understand the larger
ones eat first,
after the squirrels.
Therefore they come burdened
with gifts
knowing the center
of the open mouth
is the world.

Vixen

24

He entered
what was dark
or dark while
it was not lit.
Was it the clear-cut land
that pulled him there?
which was to him forest
until it collapsed
and anger
there was so much of it
on this world
so much sound
of it there
when disrupted
nothing of the furnitures and lawns
the chimneys he climbed into
leaving his deer on the roof
the only stop—
ice from being sold
the little forests of the world cut down.

Dancer and Prancer

25

What do they do
when he was in the house?
Do they make deer sounds?
Do they question where he went?
There's a bark sound down there—
Their nostrils flare,
their eyes widen.

Now there is what?—
scrape sound?
What should?—

They are waiting on an empty stage,
which a roof is—
A heavy curtain of air, the shingles nearly blank with age.
The emptiness, oh, it—
the breath of northern lights in the cold,
the sky-being's breath.

Dasher

The sleigh made winter a necessity
they can't underestimate
what is happening
a roof landing
as if the moon
what did they want?
light
the lifting of _______a way
into the world.

Comet

There was prophecy of cabins on the land, their
fogged breath rising from chimneys. There was
comment from the land itself, plowed and
sectioned. The windiness of the woods, the wintry
herds, all of them forgotten. The lake goes by so
fast you can't hold it, but maybe you can take one
piece here and there so all you have are hands that
are wet now and then. Even the stars make their
racket as they migrate, dragging their tin cups, their
canteens through the air.

Cupid

The hodgePodge they gave us for our
sLogging camps—
Do I have that straight?
A slide-show presentation— woodshed, saw
in snowcamp
the Plastic
Manger
here
have we
learned
Enough
your world?

They thought of their own songs and utterances as acts of identity in much the same way they attributed those acts to sounds of thunder and rustling leaves… Eighteenth-century Anglo-Americans sought to colonize or incorporate Native American soundways into their outworn beliefs for the previous century. In doing so, they translated a First Nations belief in thunder as an unintentional act of a thunderer into a belief that the thunder was the voice of God.

Richard Cullen Roth, *How Early America Sounded*

29

By saying this I am saying

A thistle was in the buffalo's fur
he ran by the thistle bush
by which I am saying he ran
too close to the bush
and caught a thistle in his fur
it was the only thistle bush on the prairie
how could he not see?

In the winter
he was cold
I'm telling you this
a thistle could not keep him warm.

The loggers cleared the land of trees
the buffalo had everywhere to run into
the only thistle left.

Morse Code

The Maker shuts his oven
closing heat from the air.
Tell me what they say—
the trees no longer holding off the sun
though it gets through
like soldiers from an old war
saying the heat-lightning of artillery fire
the thundering tanks—
that messenger
clicking his metal shutter against the small, round light.

The Dock

The first time the world was broken
those who made it happen
asked that it not happen again.
They tore cloth from the Maker's table for clouds
and wrapped the earth.
They cut the legs off the Maker's table
and buried them in the mud as logs
so the new people could walk here and there,
and the earth could shift under the heavy load
of the next world it carried.
Those who broke the world the first time
hid the power to do it again,
leaving the instructions buried
though the new people would dig and dig for them.
Someday they will find them
and there will be silence a moment,
like gravel on a dirt road before a car disturbs—
a lake before a boat breaks into the ripples—

Buffalo gets wings

How many winters
he tried running and leaping
off the buffalo jump
but only fell to the ground
he had hoped for flight
his whole life he wanted
a propeller like a helicopter
he held up his tail
when he ran
thinking of the blade
whirled above his head.

Suite for Snowplow

The earth was a dream
just floating above some dust.
the dream would have remained dream
but it longed to become a storm.
The dust did not want to mix with the dream
but the longing of the dream continued.
The dream became the storm it wanted to become
in the emptiness of being.
The dust held rigid
until it began to itch
like one of those wool coats in the mission school.
It blew into the center of the dream
that became the storm from which the earth stepped.

Shawnee Indian Mission[8]

I continue my fieldnotes despite the
furlough I have taken the weather the
antagonism of the tribes I am trying to
record. Those who have been converted are
the most difficult. I expected them to be
different. They have taken Biblical names
or names from Biblical passages. I could
not dissuade them but wrote what they
said. Did they pick up my disdain? Their
names:
Deuteronomy
Camels-four-hundred-and-thirty-five
Chushanrishathaim
Hodijah
Hallohesh
Hashhub
Now-Ehud-Made-Himself-a-Dagger
Horses-seven-hundred-and-thirty-six
Magormissabib
Mules-two-hundred-and-forty-five
Nekoda
While-lifting-up-their-hands.
They have taken names for their
tribes: the Amorites, Canaanites,
Hittites, Hivites, Jebusites,
Moabites, Perizzites, Pirathonites,
Trilobites. I told them I was
encouraged with their progress.

---

[8] Johnson County, Kansas, 1839-1862, Shawnee Methodist Mission and Indian Manuel Labor
School.
Nearly 200 students enrolled. Classes are six hours a day. On Saturday teaching is limited to
three hours. The boys work on the farm. The girls wash, cook, milk: "The girls are perfectly
quiet… I live in a stately brick house" (Miss A. Archbolt, teacher, 1850).

After half a year I heard the minifter
preach this, That Chrift, his death is of
infinite value, but our death is little
worth… Next time the Minifter came,
hee asked what I remembered… and I
did remember it… I believe Chrift
dyed for finners…
Elder Heath propounded this Queftian
[Nifhobkou] in the year of our Lord
1659
The fifth day of the fifth Moneth

John Eliot,
A further Accompt of the Progresse of the Gospel

37

Feldspar

> [a] flame sets the mountains on fire.
> Psalm 83:14

> The scene faded and all that remained was a back-
> drop of slowly falling stars.
> "Discarded Scene," *Elderberry Flute Song*, Peter Blue Cloud

They wanted sons, Elizabeth and Mary, and they
had them. The one they saw beheaded, the other,
crucified. John never did wear the right clothes; it
was that buffalo robe,[9] all that pemmican[10] he ate.
With Jesus, it was the words he said: *God can turn
stones into children he likes better than you.* The followers
puzzled how evil stuck to the shadows of the
human heart: *I spy. I want. I take.* What pebbles the
boys danced across dusty streets until a woman[11]
left her husband and married his brother, and John,
not recommending it, sat himself by Disaster. His
head on a platter. This John, Elizabeth's son. And
where was cousin Jesus, telling everyone they were
whited sepulchers? Who hasn't heard worse in these
cross-cultural cross-currents? But Jesus, Mary's son,
went to the cross, which was a Volcano. His voice
always ignescent. He set the mountains on fire with
his teeth.[12] *So nice to see you at the plane like this:*
Elizabeth and Mary in conversation— in the 15th
year of Tiberius Caesar when Pontius Pilate was
governor of Judea. After a latter spewing of the
ashes, we flew, once, over the crater,[13] some saying,
now it is dormant, but I wouldn't bank on it.

---

[9] camel-hair coat
[10] wild honey and locust
[11] Herodias
[12] arrows— Deuteronomy 32:22-23
[13] Mt. St. Helens

Basalt

> The mountains quake before him.
> Nahum 1:5

> …out through the smokehole into night.
> "Why, Coyote, Why?," *Elderberry Flute Song*, Peter Blue Cloud

We made teepee hide drawings painted vermilion—
warriors with belts on their loins and feather
bonnets[14] on their heads.[15]   The teepee the shape
of a small volcano with its vent, its smokehole. We
drew every form of creeping things and beasts on
the wall.[16]   Because the animals knew, we drew
them on the teepee hide. The stork in heaven the
turtle, the crane, the swallow knew, but my people
do not know.[17]   It was on the road to the Volcano,
before the take-off, we saw *ignis fatuus* [18] at
Wounded Knee Creek. Once even he wrote on the
ground the only letter he wrote [his hide drawing?
his petroglyph? as [i.e.] in ground-writing at
Peterborough petroglyphs [Ontario] and Jeffers
petroglyphs [Minnesota]. He didn't know water
would hold him up. The fishermen can tell you how
walking on water as if a sea of glass he must have
seen it that way. Now this was another saying of the
Holy One they took in and out of battle. At the
Early Church of the Living Volcano / the teepee on
the open prairie from the vent of its smoke hole /
or think of beating a lamb until its wool was red.

---

14 flowing turbans
15 Ezekiel 23:14-15
16 Ezekiel 8:10
17 Jeremiah 8:7
18 a light seen at night moving over swamps

Pumice

> And many graves were opened and many bodies… that slept arose,
> And came out of the graves after his resurrection, and went into the
> holy city and appeared unto many. Matthew 27:52-53

> When asked, "Just what is night anyway?"
> Coyote closed his eyes, placed his burden basket over his
> head and began making the sounds of hoot owl.
> "The Burden Basket," *Elderberry Flute Song*, Peter Blue Cloud

What do you think of the little rumblings, the
discontents, the warpings of fault lines and fissures?
What seems to be said takes some thinking. He led
captivity captive.[19]   Now that he ascended, what is
it but that he also descended first into the lower part
of the earth.[20] What could it have been to descend
into the earth: the magma and lava / the dark heat
nearly sweat lodged there? Was it where he
wandered with his ash bucket, his firepans and
shovel after Calvary, after the graves were opened?
What did the dead do the three days he was in Hell
preaching one last chance to the *unchanced*? Did
they look at one another and didn't quite know
what to do? Maybe some saw their families on the
street and weren't recognized. How had they
changed that they didn't know them? It would have
been too much anyway for the families to know
their dead were only waiting on Jesus and had three
days to kill and would have to leave again for a
second parting while the families were still grieving
from the first. Still others hid out, pulling their
tunics and cloaks and head cloths about them,
holding their little angers, the mistreatments, the
rapes, the robberies, and waited on the edge of
town for him to return from Hell and take them in
the air.

---

[19] Psalm 68:18
[20] Ephesians 4:9

Ethnology Drawer #2, File 145

This odd report came to us on its own. We don't what it means, but record it anyway as if any importance to anyone. It was an occurrence in one of the mission schools. The particular school is not named. The note was found in a priest's files who traveled to several schools and probably made the note for later puzzlement, though what he concluded is not recorded, nor the year, though it would have to have been before 1927. It seems one Christmas in a blizzard they saw Jesus wrapped in an Indian blanket in the manger. In the night they heard his cries. Out of the cold came a fox, a coyote, a buffalo. Even a cutthroat trout. They just entered the small chapel through the walls as if the walls were not there at all. Their breath steaming upward into the cold. How had this come to be? That he would appear to them in their own way? That he would be found among the prairie animals? What faith the schools hoped to build. But always falling back on anger beat them who continued to speak their old language that would hold them back from this world. The language gave them a footing and it is known we have to unfoot.

Voices from the driven world (1)

The weight of explorers, cavalry, settlers, teachers,
missionaries with the stars crooked in their heads / their
words we were able to believe despite the ash they covered
us with / they persuaded us of their way. Even after the
slaughter of buffalo and tribes the gospel brought / we were
open to what they said and said what should be said in this
darkness we are in.

The Pillion

She was from the other culture— madness. The European *comers*, of the family of garden roses but something awry the daying red, the greenblack leaves, the stems. They had their zealot who grew overwired with this right to the land and somewhere reason stubbed its toe. She made watercolors of cut, flamboyant roses formed before she disappeared in a home in St. Joseph, Missouri. No one seemed to know after that. My uncle by marriage, his mother's brother's daughter— she drew bright roses that stuck like the bitter powder of redjello before mixing into boiling water. And somehow painting she was set ablaze and there was no calming her camouflaged bloodrops, the bloating of dark night on the rim of the late-day heat— her red hot roses gripped with no outlet. She knew how the artist, held too close to the flame, was scorched until she was driven to the St. Joe home for the insane. My uncle's uncle's daughter, his niece, no, cousin— but Grace knew something other than grace as she knelt in the trough of thorns and ecstatic roses overflown in persimmon, primrose, redblack— the spidery leaves, curling tendrils, bent stems. The wild, unstoppable madness in an unfair vivid— yet her name, GRACE FIELDS stood rigid in the lower corner. Her courage in riding second seat to madness— a slice of dry ice she put her brush to, taking her erratic fieldnotes in red.

Indians and Cowboys / Cowboys and Indians[21]

In his photographs, cowboys ride horses shooting at Indians
of course— those old cast-iron figures we lined up on the
hardwood floor. I am holding a child who sees someone I
don't. In fact he's talking to him— I say who?— and he just
talks. He isn't fearful, but I am holding him. In the
photographs, there are blurred images of cowboys on horses
shooting. Why he always thought of monsters in the shape
of something indescribable he couldn't say as we talked at
breakfast of his night which had become mine as an outsider
to the atrocities of the dark. The warfare here and elsewhere
running blobs he draws on paper. It is always about the
eruption of good and evil. The old Saturday matinees, Red
Ryder gloves, cowboy shirts and chaps, the kerchiefs, the
roping tricks, the stagecoach leaving the local livery.

---

[21] David Levinthal (1949-   ), Jan Weiner Gallery, Kansas City, Missouri

They wouldn't stay dead

We played cowboys and Indians but the cowboys
wouldn't stay dead. They arose again and blew
smoke from the vent of their cap guns. Pow. Pow.
We played Indians and cowboys and the Indians
wouldn't stay dead. We learned to arise and blast
from our smoke signals the little messages / the
fieldnotes from our view of the world.

I want to get to something I remember

Someone was late to a family gathering
and the sky thundered
as though the two were connected.
Long ago
in a place
where the old relatives came,
Great Aunt Maude, Uncle John,
grandparents, others,
a great many of them.
Everyone is gone now.
I have lived alone for many years,
traveling distant places.
In my own family,
I married
and had a house in the city
I wasn't a part of.
I couldn't find the way into it.
I didn't want to find a way.
I was a distant room in the house.
The one who didn't want to be there.
Where did I want to be?
What did I want?
To be at that intersection of family
driving in the thunder
of someone else coming.
That waiting arrival.
That arrival waiting.
As though the two were connected.

Thoughts mid-flight to the fish below

They didn't like the light because it was not
in them. It was other than they were. It
lighted them with something they didn't
know. It pushed them into a smaller place.
The light bullied. The light was tool. It
shoved its light that was not wanted. They
wanted their own light, which was darkness
to us. What is light but a word? The light
burned. The light bolted. The light was
defined by light. The darkness did not
speak on its own terms, but was defined by
what was absent. The light butted the
darkness. The darkness is a tent. The light
is storm. They wanted to hold their
darkness strung with sea-beans and not let
go. What is light but a plane above the
water? What is light but a glistening wing?

Or I can answer like that Iroquois *sachem* who was pleased in Paris by nothing more than by the cook-shops.

Immanuel Kant, *Critique of Judgment*

Wyandotte County Historical Society and Museum
Bonner Springs, Kansas

They are gone now, the Hopewell who came to
Kansas 2300 years ago. They were mounds builders.
Their first artifact found in Ohio on the farm of a
man named Hopewell.

They lived in Kansas 500 years, and disappeared for
an unknown reason, probably assimilation into the
Mississippians who came after them.

The Wyandotte County Museum says *our* Hopewell
came from Ohio and Illinois, following waterways
west.

They made clay pottery with crosshatched rims
around the mouth of their jars. They grew marsh
elder, squash, corn. Gathered goose foot, walnuts,
berries, wild grains. They had a trade network for
the conch shells, pipestone, mica and obsidian
found at their sites.

The Hopewell left bone fishhooks, polished flint
balls, shells, pipe bowls, a bow-tie ax, stone ax
heads, bone awls, worked stones, spears and knife
points, mortar and pestle, stone scrapers, hoe-heads,
spade-heads, fragments of a turtle shell bowl. It's
the lists that make the clan.

In the museum case, there's one skeleton of a dog,
his head pillowed on a small limestone rock, his legs
folded under him as if running. Two worked stones
point to his chest. A hunting dog, a brave dog,
buried in ceremonial manner because the Hopewell
believed they took their possessions with them to
the next world. The curved bones of the partially
unearthed rib cage like staves of a miniature
Conestoga. The little dog running after, still
trying to make it to the next world.

Log Walkers

> If you have to read it, you don't know it.
> Vi Hilbert, Salish Elder

Where they come from?
Words with sawblades leveling
their lumberjacks oiling rungs of the sleigh
float logs in river
a spilled box of pencils
the paper
writing this.

Paul Bunyan Series

He broke the trees— Psalm 105:22

The ox could eat
a bale of hay
was it?
A bale with the barbed wire still around it

The lumber camps were soldiers
surrounded by trees
they were dreams of logs
sliding downhill
to the river

At night
the ghosts of felled trees haunted
the loggers
they heard the roots
longing for their trees

Paul Bunyan was born in a bunkhouse
the whole house
his crib
Paul Bunyan had to be bigger
than the logger's fears

A full moon with the forest still on it—
Are not the shadows on the moon
a forest growing there?

The snow was wetness with its water in remission
the falling trees
the saw blades that let blue down
to the floor of the woods

A pine needle falling there

The trees so many of them
(10,000,000)
they couldn't see through
or move without a tree in their way

In George Morrison's *Surreal Landscape, Leaping Figures,*
pen and ink on paper, 1984, (George Morrison, 1919-2000,
Chippewa) National Museum of the American Indian,
Washington, D.C.
His drawings (Morrison's): shore, water, sky
jagged brown dish-rags flying (which were logs).
He folded them together— pulled them apart—
His narratives— the pieces between the figures
of abstract shapes.

This blunt work
the loggers felled

Pine City is not pines anymore
but blue standing blueness in the air
the supine blue now floating on level ground.

He was late to math class
 10,000,000 trees
-10,000,000 trees

This clue

Our river full of trees
the whole forest
those trees cut from the ground
their roots holding the emptiness there
the history of our race—
lumberjacks all of us.

Voices from the driven world (2)

These boat-riders these wagon-riders their ships to wedge through:

Ga-do u:-s-di tsa-du:-li?-(a')? [What do you want?]

A-l'-s-go'-l'-di-ke- a-le'-w(i)-s-doh-di a'-ha-ni'
[Is it all right to park here?]

I-tsi-sv:-s-di-gwu, ni-tso'-ta-nv'-na-yi-gi'.
[You're welcome to camp but don't light any fires.]

Ha'-tlv yi-ga-su-hv-ga? [Where can I fish?]

O:sa-ni' u-do:-tlv a-su?-di a ma-y(i) di-ga-n'-di'-sv.
[There is good fishing across the water.]

Ha'-tlv i-tsi-u-di-ga tsi-yu? [Where can I launch a boat?]
Ha-la'-yv wu'-s-ta e-quo'-ni? [How long is the river?]
Ha'-tlv (go:tlv) ga?-di a-ki-hwa-hi'-s'di-i(i)?
[Where can I buy bait?]
Ha'-tlv (go:-tlv) ga-no-hi-li-da'-s-d(i) go-we'-li ga-ne-s-di-i?
[Where can I get a hunting license?]
Ha'-tlv (go:-tlv) a-hwi di-ga-dv'-di-(i)?
[Where can I weigh my deer?]

Combs Cherokee – North Carolina

Collected by Dr. Frank Speck and John Witthoft, 1932-1940
University of Pennsylvania Museum of Anthropology and Archaeology

He carved for me
from bone or horn or wood or tortoise shell
these combs for my long hair
they are *a-li-ta-wo-sdi*
these combs combing for me my hair
these combs using their teeth for me
these holy ones who take nothing for themselves.

Ledger

Who writes this book? What eruptions these?: [I owe you.]
Gv-tu-ga. [I owe you.]
[how much?] *ha-la' iga?-(i)?* The trade store takers say their ledger book says
owe for staples: barrels, shelves,
the table of dried meat that's our rationing
their sums are the edge of wind that takes how much owed underneath the
counter brought up when they see the potatoes, flour a pound half.
a-gwa-du'-li a-ki-wa-hi'-s-di-i
[I want to buy or I-want I-to-buy or I-to-buy I-want]
a-gi-lv:-k'-w'-di a ki-wa-hi'-s-di-d-i
[I like to buy or I-like-to-buy or I-to-buy I-like]
ge-li-a a-ki-wa-hi'-s-di-d
[I am thinking of buying or I-think I-to-buy or I-to-buy I-think]
di-ga?-di [buttons]
di-yv'-gi [needles]
a'-s-di [thread]
ga-tsi-no:-s-da [straight pins]
di'-l'-s-toh-di [scissors]
u-tsi-lv [cloth]
u-tsi-s-da-lu-gi'-s-g(i) [shiny cloth]
da-wi'-s-ka-ge a-hnu-wo [slick cloth]
a-tli-lo:-s-toh'-ti [tape-to-measure-it-with]
di-li-yo?-(i) [socks]
di-li-ye-su-lo [gloves]
*di'-l'-s-que'-*t(o)-wo [hats]
di-yah-tlv-di [neckties]

The Capitalistic NoteBooks

Since my correspondence with you last year nothing
has changed. We need victuals. My father, we are
hungry. Our hearts are lumps of clay. We walk back
and forth in the room and do not know where to
sit. How do I set my table in the wilderness?— as
Maschil asked in Psalm 78. Yet you provided quail
that fell from the sky / and manna. Flail us with it,
father, fall it from above that we have what we need
/ we ask only for our little ones / some for
ourselves and our old ones. You are distant and
withholding / we plead / we are sad / we cry / we
are angry / we rage because of the place we are in.
What have we done for this to deserve? They have
the advantage over us / they have all we cannot
own nor buy anything. They ask us to be
subservient which we are. They have broken the
treaties every one we hear of. We ask ownership.
We ask to produce the best Indian moccasins and
tradegoods for the cheapest price and work the
competitive market. But they mass produce our
trinkets. Kitsch. All of them. We rumble. We invent
gaming machines. Until we see their coins coming.

Lay siege against, it, and build a fort
against it, and cast a mound against it—

Ezekiel 4:2

"Who would have you for a
husband?—You with thick eyebrows,
you with your eyes full of sleep?"

from *The Owl and the Long Tailed Duck*
Report of the Fifth Thule Expedition 1921-24,
The Danish Expedition to the Arctic North
America in Charge of Knud Rasmussen,
Gyldendalske Boghandel, Nordisk Forlag,
Copenhagen, 1932

Wigwamming

This way —> to the wigwam
wiguoam
wikuwam
gowah
guuaha
which are ways of saying, *shelter.*

A wigwam is a half moon.
Or an igloo that is not ice.
A beaver mound.
Or bent saplings covered with birch bark.

Our field trip overflows with history.
We think of assimilation, acculturation,
which is to know in flood the river has access
to the land
transferring into our lives
its fish ~ ~ ~ ~
into our trees.

Wigwam (1)

> He felt an uncomfortable sensation in this throat.
> Perhaps his throat was struggling with words.
> Barbara Guest, "The Cough," from *The Confetti Trees*

Instead of trailers the director wanted wigwams on
the set.
He peeled birch bark.
He soaked saplings in the river until they bent and could form
the rounded frame
like a half moon on the ground, flat side down.

He brought from the museum
snowshoes
a string of artificial trout
animal skins stretched on a rack
scrapers, instruments and tools.

The filming of the film called *Wigwam* is in
production.
The crew is ready. The buffalo are herded onto a
prairie.
The pages of the script are learned.

The pines stand beside the lake.
The Indian flute begins.

It seems that music was the water of the film.
The trees and landscape the words.
The buffalo were anguished to see the earth as it had been.
They wept tears shiny as celluloid.
They retreated and could not be found.

The bears and beavers and muskrats and wolves
howled all night. After an hour of shooting, it was the next day.
The animals were restless. The Indians
uncooperative.
Concessions could not be made. It was too lateral.
All intentions were taken. Wrong characters showed up.

The management was unreachable.
A long tailed duck was shot while passing.

It was all behind schedule. Over budget.

Wigwam (2)

How the body hurts after its wounding
long into the   night
it speaks of its wounds
remembering the wounding
the effort   to rise
to risk being rolled into a ball that circles like a moon.

We had hoped
there was a passage from   a way out,
at least a corridor between
where a prairie starts to end
but therein   spaces of houses
gathered   square or some nearly square.
Their closets, ceilings like a hand
here in the corner the rooms so nearly.

Wigwammer

> It turned out that midway into *Hiawatha*
> she had converted to Social Realism.
> Barbara Guest, "*The Vanished Library,* "from *The Confetti Trees*

You are out there on your own
and your own is not there.
The buffalo hiding from their places
the settlers coughs
in the catalogue
orders not yet sent
or shipped as far as the prairie.
They had come so far in ships and wagons
running with their legs away.

Casting

…the buzz
of chaos in the hive, the agitation
of the workers in their cells, the veiled
figure come again to rob the combs—
Eleanor Wilner, *Field of Vision*,
from THE GIRL WITH BEES IN HER HAIR

The buffalo hides piled on the ground
higher than a man standing in a wagon
that held receipts to all that had a hand
in coffee tins
between the boards and mattresses
wherever they could hide.

The call came to help
can you come?—
I rush from what I'm doing.

It was an ungainly lot
this absurdity of a travois without wheels
that carried us across the prairie.

In boarding school we made these cardboard mounds—
beehive
hornet's nest
beaver mound
a pile of buffalo hides
the half moon in the sky—

Parking in the Village

> A need to film nostalgia crept into the studio—
> Barbara Guest, "Nostalgia," from *The Confetti Trees*

Film is a visual aspect of language. It is what is film.
Image is the first language that began in cave drawings.
The firelight filmed, making moveable the static animals
by firelight moving along the wall.

Filming the oral tradition is hearing this backdrop.
One voice 2 voices 3. Something in relationship
to the other.
Not just another, but an oppositional other.

The very work we are doing is something with scripting.

The invisible world moves beneath the dialogue.
How the disparate commune.
They are the set pieces of dialogue.
A film is a rock formation.
An association with dreams and their properties.
A film is a series of articles on a shelf.
The voices travel to an associative dialogue in the distance.

Now a figure comes near.
How words create the necessary linkage.
A migration of plot and point of recognition on arrival.

The act of filming is the establishment of this agency.
The little wigwam of the film is the fort against it.

I learned how a little film is a wigwam.
And why the making of it is called, shooting.

Wigwammed

The shortness of fundage
was a fact we often faced.
How it led to a flashback.

Finding shape was
the method we finally uncovered.

It was mostly stand and waiting
on the set
all jello and bagged pie.

We sat in chairs the heat was unassuming
but present.
Sweltering Summer was the Indian's name
who stalked the battle camp.

On Location

The wind shall shepherd all your shepherds—
Jeremiah 22:22

On the set we had closed   an invaluable cast and
crew were there   to say   what lights the gaffers
presented to us as light   and shot   what was our
film.   It was exuberant and industrious.
Uninformed as an occurrence, but otherwise an act
of contrition. We were at the table   talking   what
was   script. It was hard to remember and several
retakes later   they handed us a reminder   the
director himself seemed *blown*. I don't know how
else to say it. His words went one way   then
another   all the seedlings he had planted came up
in another direction than what he had planted. Or
thought he had   as was sometimes the case. It
was   those wigwams   he wanted. They were out
of character with what he was trying to do which
called more for the plains Indian   rather than the
woodland. There were mounds builders on the
plains too. Only they made earthen mounds instead
of bark covered   which was the effect he wanted.
Who knows what anguish he went through?   We
saw him pacing   the wigwams. A whole series of
them   wondering where he was going   who
exactly was moving his world. Why had there not
been re-writes   before shooting   why had we   not
known where   we were going with the film
before filming?   Often the   fog on the morning
air delayed shooting   we sat at our wigwams and
ate wild rice and   talked of whatever news was
there   and called to   the bears of the   wildness that
showed up occasionally mainly to go through our
trash. Had they not known   we had more food   hid
in trees   but found that bears could   climb trees
even the barest   of them.

Wigwam (3)

The heat is given a further tonality when a cloud of bees swarms over the
horizon.
Barbara Guest, "The Tear," from *The Confetti Trees*

It was resolution we sought
at the end
was what eluded

| | | | | | | | | | | | |\\\\\\   the Indians leaning against the upright
wall of the fort

the wagon
tracks==

the bee swarm attacking from the south ``` ``````````` `````` ```````````

Wigwammest

About their howses they have commonly square plots of cleared grownd, which serve them for gardens, some one hundred, some two hundred foote square, wherein they sowe their tobacco, pumpons, and a fruict like unto a musk million, but lesse and worse, which they call macock gourds, and such like, which fruicts increase exceedingly, and ripen in the beginning of July, and contynue until September; they plant also the field apple, the maracock, a wyld fruict like a kind of pommegranatt, which increaseth infinitlye, and ripens in August, contynuing until the end of October, when all the other fruicts be gathered, but they sowe nether herb, flower, nor any other kynd of fruict.

William Strachey, *Historie of Travaile into Virginia Britannia*, 1612

The aftermath of   film
the shelter that replaced the wigwam   standing
only
in museums now
the howse
grownd   the wyld fruicts of scenes
made their historie
infinitlye
kynd.

I am like an owl in the desert—

Psalm 102:6

He fell into a trance… and saw heaven
open, and a certain vessel descending to
him, as it had been a great sheet… in
which were all kinds of four-footed
animals… and fowls of the air—

Acts 10:9-12

Horned Being

There are nights they come back as human
it's a transformation of sorts
they don't want to come
but something in them makes the change
the transference to *other*
to see what it would be to walk on nearly two legs
with antlers still on its head
buckskin on its bones
the world is always moving the last field report said
he'd discovered *changing slots*
whatever they are
it was the last we heard
but scribbled on the pages we received
one leg amputated from a trap
one hand forward, the other back
the four directions for a navel.

Vision Quest at the Comet Motel

An afternoon to kill
I went to the St. Louis Art Museum in Forest Park
where I never went when I lived there.
I sat for a while in a darkened room
watching Doug Aitken's visiting exhibit *migration (empire) –
linear version*
in which he brought animals
into an austere motel room.
The horse lifted one foot then the other
the bison also in stifled confinement
nowhere to bolt
showing discomfort in minimal movement—
This study of placement in artificial landscape.

But there was snow on the screen of the television set
to comfort them.
For the horse, a herd of wild horses running
as if a vision in the back of the brain—
a lecture on the contrast of pioneer and the aftermath of
settlement.

Then there were two large white birds
(I'm only explaining this to you)
one on each of the twin beds
until one jumped on the bed of the other and they sat together
in puzzlement.
Their vision was a flock of birds flying in a fuzzy sky
hard to differentiate from the snow on the television screen
(or were each filmed to resemble each?)—
their heads jerking one way then the other in their stress.

A flock of birds flying.
A herd of horses running.
Then visions of waterway, causeway, spillway, river, stream,
pool ripples all wing-like, snow-like
and the shimmering of pool water reflected on the motel wall.
These were the side effects.

The other animals alone as they stood in the motel room
on their own—
as if Noah forgot the other half of horse, raccoon, bison, fox, rabbit,
deer, beaver, mountain lion, hawk, elk, owl.

There were accoutrements for some of them—
For the red fox, a puzzle on the bed with russet pieces
much like the fox
restless, darting here and there,
the pieces disturbed, finally flying in the air.

For the beaver, the bathtub filled with water—
(friends with a cabin once said the beavers continually built dams in
the creek
which flooded the road and they kept tearing down the dams and the
beavers only built again in pointless repetition—)
I saw the rerun of dam-building
in the rerun of the video— *migration (empire)*
the beaver's tail like the black tongue of the cow I saw once
on my grandfather's farm.

The rabbit's ears were veined as leaves—
the similitudes coming clear.
For the deer, there were deer horns on the wall.
For the elk, the antlers on its head were television antennae.

The mountain lion was the only one who tore at its environment
pulling pillow, sheet and spread from the bed
clawing, chewing
in opposition to the others who stood with impatient passiveness
or a perturbation of not knowing what to do
where to go.
The lamp knocked on the floor as if a sun
or the light bulb of the moon.

For the snow owl, white feathers fell from the ceiling
of the motel room
as if from feather pillows
or maybe television snow.
The owl stood on the snowy bed
its throat throbbing
like the gills of a fish caught from the shimmer of a river
in this wild desolation of likeness and contradiction.

[he first artis]

He watched the animal—
the bull not noticing
as he watched
the shape of its head
the exact curve of its horn, its forehead, its jaw
but the eye the eye—
How had he studied? Had he first drawn
in the dirt?
Had he made outlines in his head before he marked
the cave wall?
Who held the torch for him?
Who lit the fire?
The drawing is a ceremony before the hunt
planning the kill
under a Maker who watches watches how the man
felt the head with his eye his eye as he waited
for the moment
the bull looked up from the grass and saw the spear.
And somewhere in his cave the Maker copied—
drawing the head of Christ with his eye
waiting waiting until he was willing to give up his life.

[he transference   ]

They came with hacksaws
and regiment
and we were delved into—

And what it meant was to be resourced
removed of one's lice.

Iowa migration wetland, late winter

The earth must be wood—
the farmhouse in the distance,
the outbuildings, woodpile,
the antlered winter trees.
The brown fields have windbreaks
carved between them.
They warp after rain
with slats of plowed furrows laid across them.
A far tree in the field curved as a horse-dance staff.
The old hayroll—
a burl from which a ceremonial feast bowl
will be carved.
The telephone poles are crosses
that rise and fall on the land.
The whole earth made of what it's not supposed to be.

At the *Ompompanoosuc*
(the place of very white stones)

I.

There were times he was lit
and the mountains caught on flame—
the blaze only visible to them
who followed.
On his feet something looked like
ice skates.
The stubble on his face resembled freezer burn.
We rode buffalo
and our wood flutes became fish in the stream
we crossed.
The blades on which he walked glistened
as we followed him
into the water
and seemed to skim under the moon.
Without opening a white page in a book
he read to us.
The pack mules trailed on a rope.
That morning
the intake valves on the motors
that propelled the buffalo
froze as we crossed
and he took out his welder's torch to open them.
The long trail of buffalo—
their wake of moonlight like a tail behind us.
Someone on the bank
skipped stones on the shimmer
still entering the water
from the weedy shore.

II.

We were at the Sagatagan
by then
along the northern border.
Icicles were our noses
though our snow boots waxed.

Among the attacks
we passed the white gravestones silently—
Lucia Fruth
17 Oct 1878
2 Dec 1878

We tried to read others
Hier Ruht— but the rest had failed
and we were white with cold as the air we breathed.

Behind us the mountains were still on fire.
Now the stars too.

She was a pillar of white stone.
She did what she was told not to do
as all others we leave behind
though they throw pebbles at us
they seem as little pecks of salt against our face.

III.

The sleet was heavier now.
We led the buffalo that snorted with confusion.
The air sparked beyond our welder's helmets.

We clothed ourselves but were not warm.
I tell you his stories were barrel fire.
We would have perished otherwise.

We continued to pass men with plumb lines and hatchets.

We arrived in bitter shape.
They looked as if we were still alive.

We could hear the generators radiating discontinuously.
We could smell the electromagnetism.

The workers asked for a field report—
A list of ones we lost.
1) The man who sank in the Sagatagan
    weighted by his parka and snow boots.
    (There was nothing we could do.)
2) The girl who drowned in stone.

He lived in a time of weather

For my great-grandfather, Woods Lewis,
whose old language was stormed by the new

Horse with green jaw
two berry eyes
drink yellow creek
kleh, kleh, he neigh.
His teeth a snarl of bailing wire.
He has a house in the village,
a rusted car for a trough.
The red wind his neighbor.
All day, tumbleweed drive speed
limit.
If he had arms he could rake sky,
find turquoise moon.
Flick his ears
are stars.

I am my own virtual parts
under this wigwam
this mound of the sky I bear.

Author

EPILOGUE (1)

The Legacy of Plains Indian Shirts
Minneapolis Art Institute

> …power is the ability to start your chainsaw with one pull.
> "Coyote, Coyote, Please Tell Me," *Elderberry Flute Song*, Peter Blue
> Cloud

This is *telling-a-story*,
This exhibit of war shirts
standing on their posts
made of hide, porcupine quills, glass beads, paint, horsehair,
one shirt with red spots as if cherries,
another shirt with a horse, red zig-zag lines painted
from its mouth,
the *spirit medicine* it took into battle.

Other *pierced* shirts honoring the dream of a warrior—
when he was hiding in a badger hole from the enemy
a pierced man told him he would make it back
to his own camp.

This is *telling-a-war-story*,
how it starts above the sky where spirits war—
His Horse Looking, Lakota, 1885, drew the whole bloody field.

Red Dog drew his horse, *Few Tails*, on his shirt— wavy lines
down its flank
for the spirit powers that rode with them.

Every tribe developed their warrior societies
1) They counted coup
2) Snuck into enemy camp to steal horses tied to their owners
   when they slept—the ropes had to be cut
    without waking the sleeper
3) Led a party into war and if the party was followed, the leader
   got behind his warriors and fought hand-to-hand
    with the enemy by himself.

It is never art, this explaining work, this making the past clear,

this work of stepping across rifts, this flame of cold,
how breath rises at death,
how even our words of peace are battered.

Afterburn

Now the neighbor pulls you on a sled.
The stillness of snow compacts houses
the way you moved over
when a relative came to supper.
The tops of clouds are crusted with snow
buckling before the shovel.
Or a dream
when the white fox of your father
sat on the edge of your bed
under a brilliant moon.
Maybe in the distance
the clouds are chimney smoke
or the steamer you took back
from the Arctic
when you woke.
The vapor trail of a plane
crosses above you
making a white road that passes
into your head.
You chop the small row of windows
as though they were glass teeth.
Sometimes you'd do anything to get back.

DIANE GLANCY is professor emeritus at Macalester College in St. Paul, Minnesota, where she taught Native American Literature and Creative Writing. She was the 2008-09 Visiting Richard Thomas Professor of Creative Writing at Kenyon College in Gambier, Ohio. Her awards include a 2009 Expressive Arts Grant from the National Museum of the American Indian, the 2008 William Rockhill Nelson Poetry Award from The Writer's Place and the *Kansas City Star*, two National Endowment for the Arts Fellowships, the 2003 Juniper Prize from the University of Massachusetts Press, a Minnesota Book Award, an Oklahoma Book Award, and an American Book Award from The Before Columbus Foundation. Glancy is of Cherokee and German / English heritage. She lives in Shawnee Mission, Kansas.

PRAISE FOR DIANE GLANCY'S WRITING

"Diane Glancy's work/words strike softly from an oblique angle that leads to another dimension. In that dimension the spirit-world of the ancestors speaks with clarity and coherence through Glancy's imagistic and surreal language. She picks at the threads and strands of a vibrant heritage leaving a multilayered weaving of images haunting like a *déjà-vu* experience."

Margarita Donnelly, *Calyx: A Journal of Art & Literature by Women*

"Heartbreak as well as triumphant inwards, these two sides of the Native American heritage are the coordinates of Diane Glancy's poetry. Her voice—whether in poetry or drama—rises strong and pure from the red Oklahoma earth."

Ivar Ivask, *World Literature Today*

"Poet, novelist, essayist, playwright, and author of more than thirty books, Diane Glancy has established herself as one of the country's most versatile and prolific writers. Distinguished by her laconic honesty, her unflinching eye, and her skillful articulation of the commonplace, she presents Native American life—especially the ways it intersects with nonnative culture—in all its complexity and nuance."

Jessica Bennett, North Dakota University, Diane Glancy site

MAMMOTH PUBLICATIONS BOOKS

Barnes, Barry   *We Sleep In a Burning House: Poems* $10

Day, Robert   *We Should Have Come by Water: Poems* $10

Glancy, Diane   *Stories of the Driven World: Poems* $14

Low, Denise & Tom Weso   *Langston Hughes in Lawrence: Photos & Biography* $15 paper, $25 hardcover

Low, Denise, ed.   *To the Stars: Poets of the Ad Astra: Poetry Project* $12

Low, Denise   *New & Selected Poems* (rpt., 2nd ed.) $15

Milk, Theresa   *Haskell Institute: 19thCentury Stories* $20

Mirriam-Goldberg, Caryn   *Landed: Poems* $12

Mirriam-Goldberg, Caryn   *Landed: Poems & CD* with Kelley Hunt $20

Schultz, Elizabeth   *White-Skin Deer: Hoopa Stories* $10

Tambornino, Pamela Dawes   *Maggie's Story: Teachings of a Cherokee Healer* $14

Two-Rivers, E. Donald   *Fat Cats, Powwows, & Other Indian Tales:* $12

Order Online:

    www.mammothpublications.com (Pay Pal)
    mammothpubs@hotmail.com

Mail Order, add $3. Kansas residents add 6.3%.

Mammoth Publications
1916 Stratford Rd. Lawrence, KS 66044

CPSIA information can be obtained at www.ICGtesting.com
Printed in the USA
LVOW061527080612

285294LV00004B/40/P